Color Me Confident

Color Me Confident

ISBN 979-8-9870551-0-6

Publicity Rights

For information on publicity, author interviews, presentation, or subsidiary rights, contact:

Dr. Marilou Ryder: drmlr@yahoo.com 760-900-0556

Jessica Thompson: rthompson22@comcast.net 978-879-9288

Book design by Nan Barnes, StoriesToTellBooks.com

Printed in the United States of America

Delmar Publishing, Huntington Beach, CA 92648

Color Me Confident

DELMAR PUBLISHING

Dear Parents and Guardians,

What an awesome time to be a girl! We know your young girl continues to amaze you with all her energy and unbelievable talents. And the good news is that today she has more possibilities and choices. She can develop her talents, follow her heart and make goals for herself even in planning her future. She is introduced to many new topics, subjects, and ideas daily.

As wonderful as it is to make those choices, it can be confusing. But, making the right choices is important. That's when you need to rely on your parenting skills to help your little girl develop good self-esteem. And The COLOR ME CONFIDENT activity book can be one piece of your tool kit.

The first years of a girl's life are critical. She will learn confidence, security, love, curiosity, and bravery. You can help her get there. As authors of the SISTER TO SISTER book series and researchers of female confidence, we've learned that parents or adults can never start too early to teach and encourage confidence building with little girls.

We are proud of empowering young girls and women of all ages. Our COLOR ME CONFIDENT Activity Book will start your little girl on her very own confidence-building path in a fun and age-appropriate manner. The activities and coloring pages will help your girl focus on who she is- a confident, capable, and persistent girl eager to lead a happy and productive life.

Best of Luck,
Marilou Ryder and Jessica Thompson

All About Me!

My Age

_____

My Favorite Color

_____

My Favorite Food

_____

My Favorite Game

_____

My Hobbies

_____

My Pets

_____

What is CONFIDENCE?

YOU
Like
Yourself

YOU
Do Your
Best

YOU
Try New
Things

What is CONFIDENCE?

  You feel liked and accepted.

  You are proud of what you can do.

  You think good things about yourself.

I will always try to find the answer.

Color Me Confident

I AM GENTLE LIKE A BUTTERFLY

BRAIN TEASER

 Spot 5 differences and color

11

self care checklist

 I brush my teeth.

 I get good sleep.

 I eat fruits & vegetables.

CIRCLE 3 THINGS I LIKE ABOUT ME!

My Hair

My Smile

My Laugh

My Body

My Eyes

My Hands

I am feeling

Complete the sentence with the word that describes how you feel right now!

Smart   Proud
Pretty   Strong

Confidence Words

MATCH THE WORDS TO THE PICTURES

 Happy

 Strong

 Love

 Courage

POSITIVE
Self Talk

COLOR THE BUBBLES OF A CONFIDENT GIRL

BRAIN TEASER

 Spot 5 differences and color

I'm the girl you want on your team.

Fill in the Vowel

sm rt

CONNECT THE DOTS AND COLOR

I know when it's my turn to shine.

FINISH DRAWING THE CONFIDENT GIRL

(AND COLOR HER!)

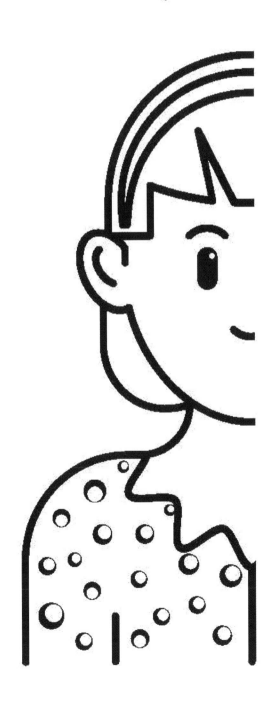

Color Me Confident

I AM CALM LIKE A SWAN

COLOR THE GIRLS WHO LOOK ANGRY

23

COLOR ME
BRAVE

I am really good at math.

Follow Your Dreams

Circle the Careers You Like

Firefighter

Pilot

Doctor

HELP THE GIRL FIND HER FRIENDS

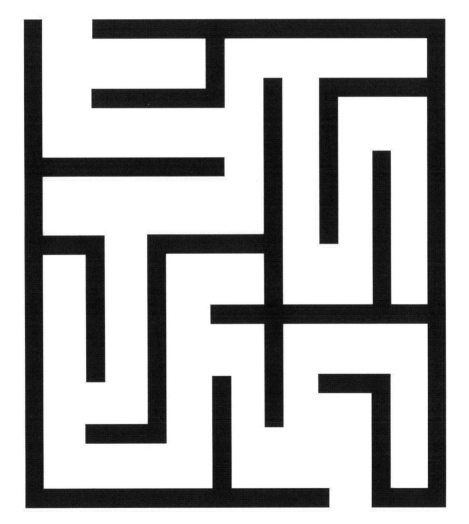

COLOR ME
PROUD

BRAIN TEASER

 Spot 5 differences

Being smart is so cool!

CONFIDENCE
COPING
SKILLS

COLOR THE GIRL THAT'S MOST LIKE YOU!

This is hard!

I need to practice!

CONNECT THE DOTS AND COLOR

I am happy and like who I am.

CIRCLE
3 THINGS I AM GOOD AT!

Singing

Reading

Sports

Cooking

Dancing

Art

Color Me Confident

I AM BRAVE LIKE A LION

I am good at

Complete the sentence with the word that describes how you feel right now!

Sports   **School**

Music   **Crafts**

Emotions Worksheet
Match the pictures and the words.

Disappointed

Bashful

Worried

Happy

HELP THE GIRL FIND HER PUPPY

Color Me Confident

I AM POSITIVE LIKE A PUPPY

self care checklist

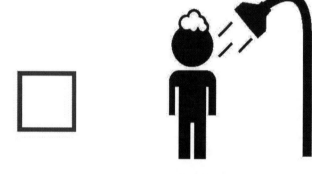 I keep myself clean.

 I take a break.

 I play outdoors.

Fill in the Vowel

pr◻ud

Follow Your Dreams

Circle the Careers You Like

Scientist

Singer

Geologist

I know how to be kind.

COLOR ME
BEAUTIFUL

CIRCLE 3 OF MY BEST QUALITIES

Kind

Smart

Curious

Honest

Positive

Friendly

FINISH DRAWING THE
CONFIDENT GIRL

(AND COLOR HER!)

CONNECT THE DOTS AND COLOR

I am bold and confident.

BRAIN TEASER

 Spot 5 differences

COLOR THE GIRL
WHO LOOKS CONFIDENT

I like to try different things.

Emotions Worksheet
Match the pictures and the words.

Thankful

Powerful

Confident

Afraid

Color it in

LOVE YOURSELF FIRST

Color Me Confident

I AM SMART LIKE A DOLPHIN

Follow Your Dreams

Circle the Careers You Like

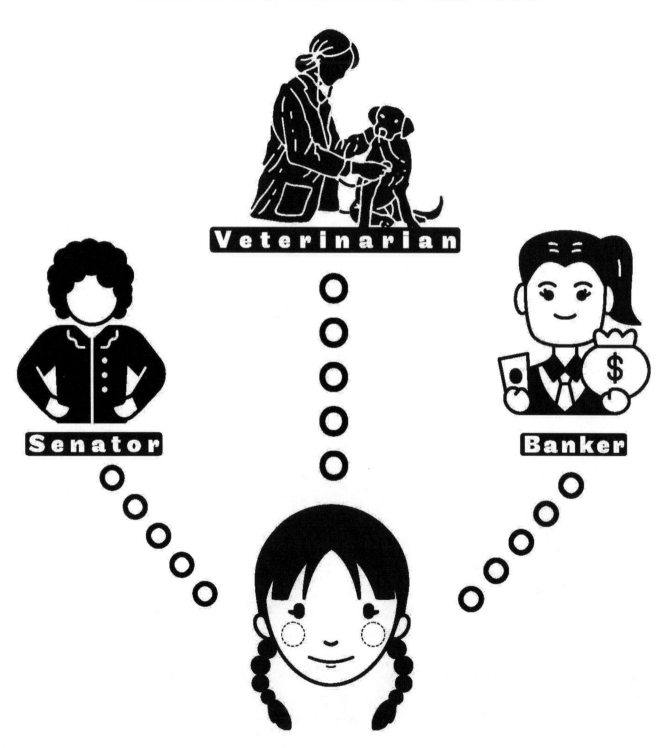

Veterinarian

Senator

Banker

When I get scared I ask for help.

COLOR ME
FEARLESS

CIRCLE 3 OF MY FAVORITE SUBJECTS

Science

Math

Reading

Writing

Music

Sports

Word Search

S	R	A	V	S	E	N	P
T	U	T	I	M	I	W	I
R	O	R	B	A	L	D	Y
O	G	R	A	R	E	S	K
N	A	M	I	T	I	O	V
G	N	B	O	L	D	C	H
B	P	R	O	O	D	A	D
N	M	E	K	I	N	D	U

STRONG   **BOLD**

SMART   **KIND**

CONNECT THE DOTS AND COLOR

Every morning I get to start over.

CONFIDENCE COPING SKILLS

COLOR THE GIRL THAT'S MOST LIKE YOU!

It's okay not to be perfect.

Follow Your Dreams

Circle the Careers You Like

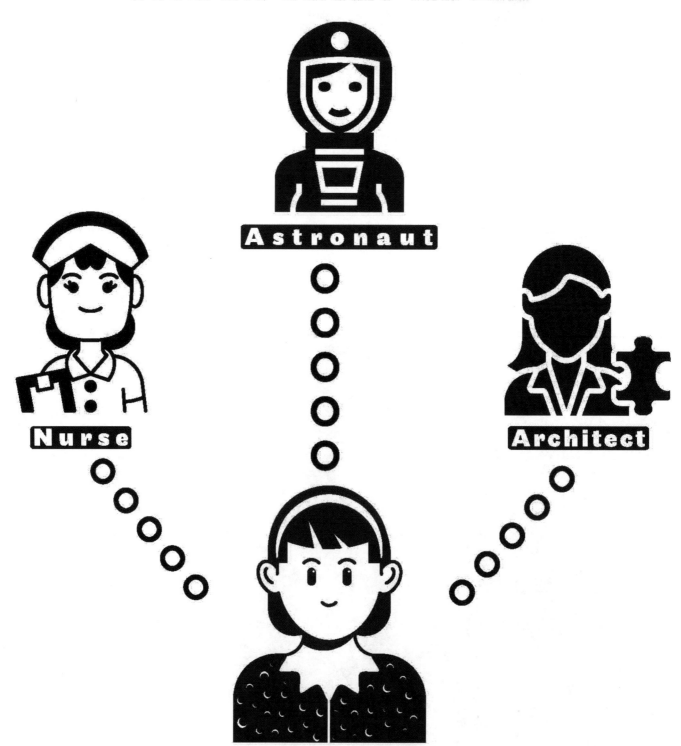

Color Me Confident

I AM BOLD LIKE A HORSE

Confidence Words

MATCH THE WORDS TO THE PICTURES

 Caring

 Healthy

 Beautiful

 Thankful

I like making new friends.

FINISH DRAWING THE CONFIDENT GIRL

(AND COLOR HER!)

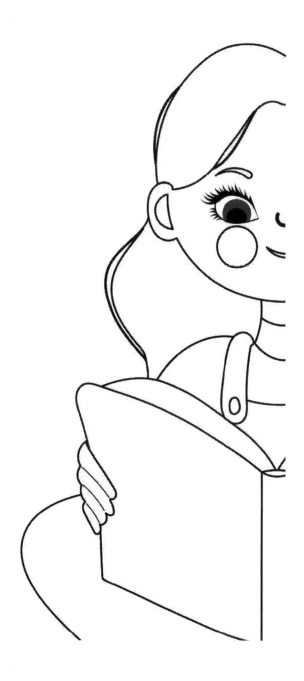

CONFIDENCE COPING SKILLS

COLOR THE GIRL THAT'S MOST LIKE YOU!

CONFIDENCE

BRAIN TEASER

Spot 5 differences

CONNECT THE DOTS AND COLOR

I am a shining star.

COLOR ME
TALENTED

I am a good classmate.

COLOR THE GIRLS WHO LOOK WORRIED

Fill in the Vowel

h_ppy

Follow Your Dreams

Circle the Careers You Like

Dentist

Pharmacist

Judge

I love to try out new hair styles.

Help the Sad Girl Become Happy

I love to learn new things.

POSITIVE
Self Talk

COLOR THE BUBBLES OF A CONFIDENT GIRL

CONNECT THE DOTS AND COLOR

I love being part of a team.

CONFIDENCE
COPING
SKILLS

COLOR THE GIRL THAT'S MOST LIKE YOU!

I am feeling

Complete the sentence with the word that describes how you feel right now!

Happy   Confident
Kind   Excited

HELP THE GIRL EAT HEALTHY

Color Me Confident

I AM BEAUTIFUL LIKE A PEACOCK

Follow Your Dreams

Circle the Careers You Like

Software Designer

Teacher

Author

CONNECT THE DOTS AND COLOR

I love to try out new sports.

CIRCLE 3 THINGS I ALWAYS DO!

Ask for Help

Take My Turn

Follow Rules

Speak Up

Enjoy Learning

Try Hard

FINISH DRAWING THE CONFIDENT GIRL

(AND COLOR HER!)

Word Search

S	R	L	E	A	R	N	P
T	U	T	G	M	P	W	R
F	R	I	E	N	D	L	I
K	G	R	A	R	K	S	D
N	A	M	I	T	I	O	E
I	N	T	E	A	M	C	I
B	P	R	O	U	D	A	V
N	I	E	K	I	N	D	E

FRIEND   **POSITIVE**

TEAM   **LEARN**

CONFIDENCE COPING SKILLS

COLOR THE GIRL THAT'S MOST LIKE YOU!

CONNECT THE DOTS AND COLOR

Some days I feel like a princess.

Color Me Confident

I AM PROUD LIKE A KITTY CAT

Fill in the Vowel

st r◼ng

CONNECT THE DOTS AND COLOR

I like to imagine.

self care checklist

 I spend time with my family.

 I make time for hobbies.

 I tell my family when I'm sad.

COLOR ME
LOVED

Draw You!

I AM A CONFIDENT GIRL

COLOR THE FACE THAT YOU FEEL NOW

Made in the USA
Columbia, SC
23 June 2024

37387544R00057